How to Analyze People

Psychology System For Speed Reading Body Language & Personality Types

Table of Contents

INTRODUCTION

In prehistoric times, Ancient men lived almost like any other animal species, in constant distrust of one another. They were mostly hunter-gatherers that rarely lived in groups or societies. Most lived solitary lifestyles that precluded any chance of meeting with others. Luckily for us, this did not continue for long. In order to beat the beasts of prey that hunted them, and to find solutions to adverse weather conditions, human beings began to learn to live as groups firstly in hamlets and nomadic groups, and then larger societies. This is the single most remarkable event that has happened to determine our modern existence. What made this possible, though? How were our ancestors able to set up new cities and begin the drive for technology?

The answer is **communication.** The only reason we are the dominant species on earth is that we have the best social groups built on communication. Man-to-man, we can converse and bring value to each other's life. We can argue and debate until a mutually satisfying solution is reached. Sadly, as sophisticated as our communication skills are, our abilities to read anything less than full and complete communication is not too developed. Therefore, we have conflicts arising from differences in thoughts, perspectives, aims, and present circumstances.

From a fellow human to another, communication transcends just verbal speech. It is a full-body exercise, but in our default state, we are built to pick only clear and obvious signs from speech, and the most obvious of body language moves. This causes a lot of misunderstandings and conflicts of purpose and intent. Often, we misinterpret our discussions with other people and spend time, money, and effort on fruitless showdowns. Other times, we get deceived and taken in because we cannot read the less-than-obvious signs.

This is why I wrote this book for you; to teach you how to analyze different personality types and pick up less-than-obvious cues and signs from the people you come in contact with. This is actually possible. Here's why. In the same way that most people do not train their mind to spot cues that can actually help form an initial judgment, most people do not realize that each time they speak, they let out a pack of cues that can easily confirm or disprove what they have just said. Your job is to learn to spot these little details and translate them into concrete, actionable data that can help you stay a step ahead of all conversations. Knowing a person's exact mental state alone gives you a huge advantage in being able to decode what the person actually wants.

Ready to read people the right way? Let's get started right away!

CHAPTER 1:
KNOW YOURSELF TO KNOW OTHERS

Trying to have a clear understanding of others is cool, but then it is of utmost importance to fully understand yourself first. A clear understanding of your being is going to give you an insight into how the internal processes work for you and, subsequently, other people. Knowing the fact that insecurities, emotions, and sentiments can alter our behavior makes us realize that this same change applies to most other people as well.

The content of this book will go a long way in making you perform a self-examination and know your own body language better before you can have a better understanding of others. Having some problem or difficulty understanding others is a clear indication that you are encountering some issues that hinders you from having a proper understanding of your internal process. Observing and noting your internal process (and its outward expression) will give you the chance to have a complete understanding of the way other people may be thinking and behaving.

Not being able to make a conscious effort to critically observe your own actions will only make you see other people's actions through the lens of your prejudices, insecurities, and fears without trying to come up with any conscious thought about the particular people. The result of these assumptions will only make things worse as it will create a false image or misrepresentation about the attitude of others.

A clear and straightforward understanding of yourself will make you see the direct and indirect effect of the thoughts of the people around you. The understanding of the kind of impact you have solely depends on how well and clear you can make self-observation. Also, it depends on how important you are to that particular person, your mode of communication, and, more importantly, how you make a presentation of yourself.

Let's take this as an example. If your actions portray you as being stern and severe, the people around you, after observing this, will try and adjust to fit in with your character. On the other hand, if you are the type that looks happy and behaves lively, people around you will also warm up to this character.

Being equipped with the right analytical skills will help you out a lot. It would mean that you can discern beyond surface emotions and understand unspoken thoughts and emotions in some instances. Learning to analyze other people may be quite confusing and time-consuming at first; however, getting reasonable improvement to sort out things is key. This will give you ample opportunity to make some reasonable judgments and predict unfolding circumstances better. Being able to analyze others will go a long way in deciding the kind of approach and relationship you build with others.

How will knowing how to analyze others help you?

- ***Self-Awareness***

If you can analyze other people effectively, your skill will not only be limited to analyzing them. Subconsciously, you will also be able to analyze your own actions even better. That means you will be more aware of your own strengths and weaknesses. Self-analysis will ensure that you are quite sure and aware of your emotions, and this will make you feel responsible and have a clear understanding of any action you carry out.

People that are self-aware will not find it challenging to convert a negative attitude to a positive one. They are always able to adjust their perceptions, admit their own flaws, and make the best out of life. Self-awareness makes you have a genuine life and builds the framework for you to hold great relationships with other people.

- ***Get Considerate***

To learn to read people, you will need to invest time and energy to understand those around you. This drive is mostly moved by the desire to make peace with them. You will learn to understand that we are all not equal. An individual who understands others will relate with people in an approachable and fantastic way; by doing this, you will learn to be more considerate. You may probably be a boss who gives close attention to his employees whenever they need help. The bottom line is that you will have a better ability to adjust for other people.

- ***Get More Empathetic***

In the process of analyzing the personality and emotions of people, you will begin to think about the reasons behind human behavior, attitude, and actions. In due time, you will figure out the most common reasons why people get upset, withdrawn, and uncomfortable. Having a clear understanding of the drive and motivation that triggers changes in people's mood is key to being empathetic. Being able to analyze the emotions of others will make you empathetic to the extent that you will be able to put yourself in other people's shoes and understand why they have particular feelings.

Empathy is a rare, positive trait that very few people are able to feel and exude. Understanding and reading others, though, can give you an insight into their emotions, thoughts, and motivation. That alone can propel your ability to empathize.

- ***Get more intelligent and organized***

Being analytical will get you prepared for any situation that might probably come up. Having a wealth of knowledge that includes other people's motivations and thoughts will leave you a data bank to guide your actions around these people. Being analytical can also increase your orderliness. You may learn to respect timed deadlines better and stay on top of your day every day.

- ***Be more successful***

Of course, one of the importance of being an analytical person is that you will get success in all your endeavors. at work, relationship, or school. Having the ability to analyze will make you dependable, considerate, and empathetic. Having those traits makes you become a great personality, and you will be able to maintain any relationship you desire. Anybody who probably meets you by chance on the street will be happy they met you and will definitely like you. Then you will be seen as an intelligent and reliable person, and people will be willing to associate themselves with you

- ***Figure out your strength and weakness***

Making self-analysis may be discouraging at times, but then, you can use it as a conscious effort to address your weakness and strength. To identify your strength, it is simply anything that you are good at doing, things that occur naturally, what you cherish about yourself, or what other people like about you.

One thing that the corporate world so much cherishes is knowing your strengths. Being able to know your strengths and adapting to fit into the skillset it promises is an important denominator in your overall business and professional development.

Figuring out your weakness is not something far-fetched. A weakness is a factor, condition, or trait that we are struggling with, and this can probably be that you don't take time to listen to some other people's opinions. It can be that you like to talk so much about irrelevant things, you may be disorganized or probably forget things as soon as possible. Irrespective of the kind of weakness you have, make sure you are not taking things too hard on yourself. Being worried about your weakness is something that can make you feel down, but then it does not stop you from living the kind of life you want. When making your self-analysis, you have to be honest, sincere, and ensure you are optimistic about the future.

- ***Analyze others Effectively***

Of course, it's of utmost importance to understand the differences in your communication and action with other people. Communication as our greatest evolutionary tool is not always by speech. Speech is the most prominent tool, but most people do not even realize that we speak with almost all of our body. Yes, that's right. Body language can be just as effective as the words we speak to one another. By knowing how to analyze others, it means you are not just relying on the words they say. You are matching their body language to the words to see if they fit. If they do, fine. If they do not say the same thing, though, then you can go further to discern the reason for the disparity and attempt to fix it.

In conclusion, learning to analyze other people has a lot of advantages. It will increase your self-awareness, help you to build bigger reserves of empathy and genuine compassion, and understand those around you better.

CHAPTER 2:
WHY THE DIFFERENCE?

Before we discuss the different personality types available, we need to look at why people have different attitudes in the same circumstances. Why is Ann selfless and Mike selfish? Why is my husband a narcissist, and how did I end in a codependent relationship? Nobody acts independently of their values, beliefs, and attitude. So, let us look at that!

Beliefs, Values, and Attitudes

To be able to understand most people, it is of utmost importance to understand values, belief systems, and attitude. This will go a long way to explain their behavior and also give you a better perspective on different personality types.

Values are a set of moral rules to which great importance is attached. They serve as a determining factor to the standard you give yourself and the things you find important in life. The main reason why these values are put in place is that it's going to uphold education, spirituality, equality, and honesty. Negative traits like prejudice, hate, anger, dishonesty, frustration, and sadness have no space in a proper values system. For each of the values held by a person, there is a belief system that guides their conduct.

Your attitude refers to your average mental state that creates a link between your values and some behaviors that are attached to it. Although the importance of your attitude is great, then it is not as rigid as the value system and belief. Some other happenings can easily influence your attitude at a particular point, such as stress, and the kind of people that are around you. Attitude is flexible and hugely dependent on the particular situation you meet yourself in.

In trying to analyze someone, you need to look at their attitude and values/belief system critically. That will help you decide if a particular action/trait is a permanent feature of their character or a momentary blip due to prevailing circumstances. Why do I say this?

In trying to analyze people, you must also be conscious of the fact that the people you are analyzing are humans bound by the vagaries of their nature. That a person manifests a sign of narcissism does not make them a chronic narcissist. A selfless person this minute may turn out to be incredibly self-centered the next moment. So, what determines values, beliefs, and attitude at each specific moment?

Here are a number of core reasons guarding the development of a specific trait, character, or attitude.

Genetics

Proteins may be the building blocks of life, but genes carry the blueprints. The physical and psychological making of a human is completed first in the genes. This is why genes are the great libraries of humanity — in them do we find the first reason why people look, speak, talk, behave, etc. as they do. Genes represent one of the most significant reasons why people are what they are. So, we all pick up some of our traits and social behaviors from our parents.

Genes ensure the continuation of races, ethnicity, and families. Genes define the phenotypical traits of individuals. In some people are genes that predispose them to violence. In others are genes that condition them for kindness, gentleness, and a host of virtues. In some others, both of these traits will be found in equal proportions. But analyzing the genes of a person requires special knowledge, skills, and sophisticated equipment. So, why have I included a discussion of gene here if you will not be going around with a miniaturized lab in your pocket and taking DNA samples from people? The answer is a very simple one.

First, understanding the role genes play in defining the traits of certain individuals will help you understand why they behave in a particular way, and why it seems they are incapable of change. It will help you appreciate the nature of fellow humans, and once you do, you will learn not to worry about things too much. You will learn to forgive and forget quickly.

Second, it will help you analyze some individuals very well, especially if you are close enough to know their families. How is this so? Traits, I have already explained, are passed down from parents to offspring. Imagine, then, how the knowledge of Ted's father being a chronic drunk may help you explain that the codependent or narcissistic traits you now see in him might become full-blown someday? Imagine being able to get assurance that the kindness Jane exudes is a heritage from her dad who is reputed to be pleasant to a fault. The ability to analyze people, especially to be able to predict how they might behave now and later, will help you define your relationships with them. But who says genes alone determine the making of an individual?

Nurture, or A Lack of It
As a determinant of a person's trait, nurture is contrasted with nature. The idea is a simple one — an individual might have been born with specific

traits passed down from their parents, but the environment into which they are born and in which they are raised, may suppress such specific traits in favor of others. Numerous studies have confirmed this. A child that grows up in a violent neighborhood without any gene predisposing him to violence may end up learning this vice as a way of life. A person born with a gene that predisposes them to violence may end up being raised in a family of academics and professionals, in an environment that celebrates cool-headedness, academic, and career achievements. Such a child will grow up with such coolness overshadowing his/her natural predisposition to violence. The child's natural predisposition is nature, but what the environment it grows up in makes it is nurture.

Thus, in understanding why people are the way they are, genetics alone may not hold the key. The type of home, family, and neighborhood they grow in also matter. When it comes to humans and how they behave, both nature and nurture play important roles, and understanding this will help you appreciate a little extra information about people and understand them better.

Stress

Stress as a determinant of traits, values, and beliefs is something everyone can easily relate with. We all experience stress for one reason or another. It is the emotional pressure we all feel in differing situations. This feeling can be caused by a variety of factors. It could be from the tedium of a busy day at work or the agony of sitting in heavy traffic on your way home or the exacting nature of your partner. Stress is accompanied by a feeling of constriction — you feel like something is pressing down on you or weighing down your neck. If not properly checked, stress can lead to anxiety. But before it does, it leaves its imprints first on your personality. How?

There are three factors that link stress to one's personality. The first is the decision to go to or avoid a place that triggers one's stress. If a person has to take the train to work every day, the knowledge of the crowd, how every single space is taken, how they always have to stand, etc., might determine how they relate with others at work, on the train, and at home. They cannot avoid any of these places, so each day is a worry for them. The second is how people process and react to stressful situations. While some are fighters who never get defeated in stressful situations, others give up quickly and allow their frustrations to show quickly. Interacting with such persons during or after such a situation will reveal a side of them no one will like.

The third factor deals with the strategy people employ to cope with stress. This especially defines their personality and how they relate with others to a very large extent. Some people become reclusive when they are under intense emotional pressure. They tend to withdraw to themselves, not wanting to have much interaction with others. If you happen to be sharing space with them during such periods, they will try as much as possible to avoid you or avoid confrontation with you. If the stress persists, the coping strategy persists, and soon, it becomes a part of them to behave that way even when the stressor is out of the way later. Other people may become more sensitive than usual and go out of their way to harvest emotional pain. There are uncountable ways people devise and adopt to deal with stress; all these show up in their personality.

Previous Experience

"Once bitten, twice shy," goes the saying. "Only a fool gets burnt twice by the same fire," says another. The truth is that we are living our experiences. Like a judicial precedent, it is difficult for us as humans not to connect the dots when two situations are similar. It is human to judge our later experiences or situations by our previous ones.

Military generals rely on this simple logic in war, and so does the ordinary person on the street whose deal with a local shop owner fell through. We are all teeming with experiences, and it will be unwise not to learn from our past to shed some light on our future. This is the natural programming or philosophy we all carry in us, and that includes you. So, you are not the only one interpreting the fidgety nature of a fellow colleague as a sign that they are hiding something from you because someone else had done the same thing in the past, and they were fidgety around you. Everyone does that, or, more appropriately, the human brain does that.

A person who has been duped before, once or twice, will certainly be predisposed to distrust people. A woman who has had many failed relationships will either be careful with the next one or will care little about it. We are defined by our past experiences; only the extent of such definitions varies.

Preformed Notions about people they meet
It is impossible not to form an opinion about someone you are meeting for the first time, let alone someone you have always known. This is just our natural way of saving on processing time later. If you have to start afresh each time you meet a person, life would be difficult.

So, we collect data about people, analyze the data in our brain, make deductions from them, and store the information away. The next time we meet them, we pull out such information from the background of our mind and continue from there. It is a simple logical, and biological process. And the same way this happens to you so does it to others. People's traits, character, or attitude towards us are determined by their preconceived notions of us.

Such preconceived notions may be bestowed by our nationality, ethnicity, religion, or race. To understand how preconceived notions affect how people behave towards others, you may also want to consider switching roles –put yourself in the shoes of the person about whom an opinion is formed before they were even met, and you would understand why people act as they do.

Low Confidence

The level of confidence a person exudes is another factor that determines their character. Confidence in oneself or self-confidence is crucial in our interaction with others. Where a person holds himself or herself in low self-esteem, they tend to give in to the wishes of others quickly. They tend to be easily manipulated by others to do their bidding. A person with no self-confidence may have good ideas, but they let such ideas be shut down because they do not believe much in their own ability to come up with something good. So, rather than stand for their ideas, they just let it get brushed aside in favor of inferior ones. In some cases, they even let others take the glory for their ideas or let others push the blame for something onto them. People with low self-esteem are the perfect codependents – they are always willing to run to the beck and call of others in a bid to please these others and win their approval.

On the other hand, a person with a high level of self-confidence has a balanced personality. She does not overplay her ability, and neither does she downplay it. She understands her limitations and will honestly admit them so that she can improve. She stands for her ideas and will not suck up to anyone who rubbishes them. Such people have the present state of mind to discover those with low self-esteem and help them rather than exploit them. People with self-confidence are open-minded and will consider your views objectively. They may not agree with you, but they will respect your right to hold your view and will only attack them with much civility. They are more often than not non-belligerent.

Different Intentions and Wants

All humans are animals of opportunities and desires. From the governor who wants a new project that will take up the land of many, just to have something to show for his term in office, through the real estate developer who has been acquiring the land to be affected in hopes he might make money from development, to the person who is not willing to give up their land, we are confronted with the usual relationships of life. We are creatures of wants and competition. What one wants, the other has and does not want to lose. Thus, when we perceive others to be in competition with us, we go on the defensive, if not the offensive. We show hostility, sometimes apparent and other times, mild. The same person who appears cold to you because he senses you have the same goals may be friendly tomorrow when the goal is no longer a bone of contention between you. It is the law of wants and desires.

In the end, you will always meet many people daily who show different attitudes and emotions towards you. Some of these are mediated by factors outside their immediate control. Keep this in mind as you try to process their state of mind.

CHAPTER 3:
READING BODY LANGUAGE

As I mentioned in the last chapter, as humans, we speak to communicate. However, every one of us produces consistent communication cues using our body language aside from verbal communication. The study and importance of body language cannot be overstated. Not only must you learn to support the messages you are trying to pass with appropriate body language elements, but it is also of paramount importance to be able to decode what other people's body languages suggest.

Do not limit body language to just certain hand gestures, such as "thumbs up" gestures. These gestures are too straightforward; you also need to be able to pick up the most subtle ones that the object does not even know they are giving off. Body language is particularly important when it affects what someone means.

Even an ordinary "thumbs up" gesture can be interpreted in many ways depending on the context. Also, while talking about verbal communication, some are very similar to the body language, this is due to the fact that certain, specific actions may accompany it and possibly give them an entirely different meaning.

By the same measure, some gestures seem straightforward, and their purposes can hardly be altered; an example is when you point your finger at something. Its meaning is usually very straightforward, but then, that changes when you are pointing fingers subconsciously. That may change the meaning entirely. For this reason, it is important to be conscious of what your hands and other parts of your body are doing while you talk so that you will not drop deeper cues than you are actually willing to.

With body language, you must put some factors into consideration. These include your stance, eye movement, body movement, and facial expression. The thing is that all of these factors communicate things that we do not utter verbally, and this will give other people an idea about our feelings or what we are probably thinking about at that particular time.

Now the biggest question with analyzing body language is determining whether body language is being done unconsciously or consciously. It is always hard to make a proper connection between what is happening around us and what is being discussed. This is because, most times, we give a physical response automatically or instinctively. For most people, realization only dawns after they must have passed unintended markers to the person they are addressing.

Body language seems, for the most part, to be unintentional and instinctive such that it does not require much thinking; the topic it raises is that of the conscious and subconscious mind. Most times, our subconscious mind makes us carry out some outward gestures, and our body will reflect the things on our minds, such as feelings and longings.

In explaining this concept in a simple term, it is essential to make the clarification that our mind places its focus on the information and other factors in our environment. Although the information running in the background is vast, it is possible to go through all the information and then place focus on the parts that are of utmost importance. Of course, body language can also be carried out intentionally, and this is an indication that it is carried out by using our conscious mind.

Still though, the major part of body language is not always deliberate. We carry it out unconsciously because it is natural and mainly out of our immediate control. Many research studies claim that the most significant part of our communication is through body language rather than spoken words. There is a school of thought that suggests that only 7% of our communication is done verbally. Other researches claim that 55% of our communication is channeled through the movement we carry out with our faces, the nose, and the eye to be precise. The figures and stats may differ, but there is no doubt that the majority of our communication makes use of non-verbal communication

Of these, it is widely believed that facial expression is best to make judgment calls and decipher the moods of the people we are holding a discussion with. Again, this consensus is not general or agreed upon by all and sundry. It is important for you to be able to decipher a person's overarching emotional state through their body language. How is this possible?

Body language mirrors our emotions and state of mind. That is why you skip and bounce around when you are happy. It is also why you move around downcast when something bad happens. Of course, our emotions are shown in different ways, but then body language is a unique way of making an expression. It is something we carry out unknowingly most times. The reason is that that our hand gestures and body movement are most times carried out without prior reflection. This is very useful when analyzing a person. If they say something contrary, you will be able to figure out that they are not sincere with their utterance. You can as well use it to analyze yourself and know how your body communicates unconsciously. More importantly, you will figure out whether there is synergy between your thoughts and body language at the same time.

Body language can be very useful, most especially when you are just introduced to a new person. It is possible to get information from a person's body language even though you have not had any formal conversation; the way people hold themselves or talk can give you an inkling as to their temperament, mood, and emotions.

Elements That Impact Body Language

On this aspect, we cannot assume a general meaning for the gestures because it varies. Different people have different ways of expressing themselves physically. This can probably be intentional or otherwise. Also, cultural influence can as well affect the interpretation of some movements. The social standards are different from one culture to the other. A perfect example is "breaking eye contact." Usually, it can connote bashfulness, shyness, or some level of awkwardness. However, this is not its meaning in certain societies. For instance, maintaining proper eye contact means you are open to conversation, but in Japan, the simple interpretation is hostility and anger.

Of course, you should understand the fact that there are many things to consider when you are trying to evaluate people other than the mere usage of body language, although body language happens to be an essential basis to make the evaluation. In this book, varieties of factors are well detailed, and you can combine them with body language to have an insight into what is going on in people's minds. These factors are things you will find instrumental and will even help you when interacting with other people. They will give you more understanding and accuracy to determine the body language of people, irrespective of how delicate the situation may be.

- **Proxemics**

An anthropologist known as Edward Hall gave the first clear description of this term in 1960. Proxemics deals with the study of the space you hold between yourself and the person you are talking to. Proxemics alone can tell you how close two people are. It accurately predicts the kind of relationship between conversationalists. The general rule is that the closer you are to someone, the closer you are going to stand to them while talking.

Intentionally or unintentionally, the way we stand can determine just how happy we are in that circumstance. As a general rule, for close friends and family, we always stand not more than 1.5 - 2.4 feet away from them. A public speaker or casual acquaintance, on the other hand, may stand at distances of more than ten feet even without trying to come closer. Context is important, though.

- **Oculesics**

This is about the movement of our eyes; more importantly, how you look at another person.

Oculesics is another significant fact you have to address when evaluating the non-verbal communication of another person. In the next paragraph, the two significant subdivisions of oculesics will be discussed. Observing eye movement is necessary as it can reveal quite a whole lot.

The first thing to consider is the pupils' size, observing how they contract and dilate when your object is in a conversation with another person. Although this is a factor that you can hardly notice and is tricky considering the fact that environmental factors can influence the pupil size. The pupils can communicate fear, arousal, nervousness, hostility, and longing.

The second thing you should consider is eye contact; it has so many subdivisions on its own. Eye contact can be interpreted to be many things depending on the particular one you make. More importantly, what does your subject of analysis do when you make eye-contact with them. Do they look away quickly? Did they hold your gaze for some time? Other people may choose to look upward, downward, adopt a side-to-side movement of the eyes, stare, close the eye, blink rapidly, squint, or wink.

- **Stance and Carriage**

To complement the oculesics and proxemics, you need to watch how people place their bodies, and how they carry themselves. The way people position their bodies can give a close insight into their moods. How do you stand when talking to people? Opening up your body with a wide stance communicates confidence and surefootedness. Slouching or folding your body inwards can be a sign of nervousness or doubts. How do you shake people? Firmly or weakly? Do you clasp their hands, or do you wait for yours to be clasped? All these are factors that can help you determine the state of mind of the person in front of you.

- **Walking Style**

The way a person walks or moves can tell you a whole lot about them and their present circumstances. Think of it this way; when an infant is happy, he moves excitedly at a quick pace. He may even run until he falls down. On the other hand, when small children are angry or unsatisfied, they walk heavily with drooping shoulders and are unlikely to cover as much ground as they would if they were happy. Well, none of us ever outgrows the link between our mood and the way we move.

In the first place, under normal circumstances, everyone has a distinctive walking pattern that is easily recognizable and sets them apart from most other people. That is why you can see the back profile of your friend and know he is the one. Now, that walking style itself is a product of the average mood the person enjoys. For that reason, if you are naturally excited most of the time, your walking style is bound to reflect that. On the other hand, if you are happy and optimistic, your walking style is going to show that too.

Let us look at some common mental states and how they affect the way people walk.

Confident and Goal-oriented

Confident people often walk with what may even look like a strut. They may walk rapidly and swing their open arms around a lot. Confident people often balance a lot of their weight on the balls of their feet, and that gives them that unique bounce and explosiveness in their walking style.

Meditative

Being deep in thoughts characteristically decreases your consciousness of your immediate environment. As a result, you may walk around a bit aimlessly, hold your index finger to your mouth frequently, and give little starts when you happen upon a new train of thoughts. You may kick a stone on the sidewalk or take little rests to resume your aimless stroll as you process new information or struggle to decide. Another common sign is clasped arms behind your back. It usually denotes heavy thoughts and reflection over a decision.

Critical and Secretive

Critical and secretive states of mind often feature bowed heads, furtive glances around, and arms stuck deep into pockets while walking. People who are like this often have little frowns and take wary glances around them from time to time. They are hardly the greatest of talkers, and they listen more than they speak.

Troubled or Dejected

It is normal to have a heavy heart when we are dejected or troubled. At such times, you may walk with heads bowed and your mind seemingly off the road in front of you. It is not infrequent to collide with things or bump into people coming from the opposite direction. This is because you may not necessarily be aware of your surroundings. When you notice someone seems to be walking in this manner, the chances are that they are worried sick about something. Add to that deep frowns, and you have a confirmation that they have something furiously disturbing them.

- **Handshakes**

Handshakes are a common feature of daily interaction as a form of formal and informal greeting and acknowledgment. Handshakes can go beyond just that, though. They can also help you to process the personality type of the person in front of you.

Our personality and attitude carry through in everything we do. Therefore, even the way a person shakes other people can tell more about his own personality. In fact, choosing to shake hands or not can be illuminating just as much as they type of handshake. Why do I say this?

Say, for instance, that a person ignores a stretched-out hand and hugs the other person instead. That could constitute an admission of more familiarity than expected. Especially for women, this is also a constant occurrence in times of grief and crisis. Usually at such times, even when the hand offered is taken, it may be a bit different from the usual handshake. It may be taken between two palms, with one hand interlocking with the offered hand.

Ignoring the hand, however, can communicate rudeness, contempt, or outright rejection of the person offering the handshake. It could be an acknowledgment that you are not satisfied with the person's conduct or even a form of outlet for your anger.

Handshakes originated from the old Roman custom of holding up both hands to show that there was no weapon or harm intended to the receiver. In modern times though, handshakes come in different forms and formats, and may even be affected by location and local customs. So, there is no single, generally accepted form of handshake worldwide. For instance, Germans pump hands once; and the French shake hands upon entering and exiting a room.

However, the ideal handshake is firm and solid. It should feature you grasping the other hand, allowing your hands to interlock briefly and then stiffening the hand in a symbol of oneness. What are the things that can go wrong with a handshake, though, and what may they suggest?

A clammy hand often signifies nervousness, especially when the weather conditions do not really support perspiration. Sweating is one of our natural responses to stressful situations. Unfortunately, it can show up in your handshake. A limp handshake signifies a lack of confidence or enthusiasm. A limp handshake could be because the person is overawed or overwhelmed by a developing situation or even starstruck. It could also be a form of showing you are not very interested in meeting the person in front of you. The ultimate form of disdain can be expressed through handshakes by immediately withdrawing your palm the moment the other person takes it in theirs. That shows what you think of their touch. Another way is by offering the tips of your finger instead of the entire palm for someone else to shake. Watch out for these little things as you attempt to judge someone's impression about you when you offer your hand or take theirs in a handshake.

CHAPTER 4:
UNDERSTANDING PEOPLE'S OUTWARD PERSONALITY

To understand the outward personality of people, this chapter will be particular about four facets that will help you in understanding people's lifestyle and personality.

At that moment when you meet a new person, the simple truth is that there are lots of things you don't know about them. All you have to go on at that moment are the outward clues you can pick out; their choice of clothing, physical appearance, speech pattern, and gait, for instance. In addition, you can also try to know more about people by watching the kind of people they mix with, their interactions with them, their social life and tastes. All these combine to form a mental image of the person's character profile within your mind.

In evaluating people, it is of utmost importance to be objective so that you do not just jump into preconceived conclusions. Most times, one sign is not enough to ascribe a particular character trait permanently to an individual. You need an aggregate of complementing attributes to reach such definitive conclusions. In fact, it is not advisable to reach a conclusion based on just observable traits and remain unyielding to contrary signs later on. Your conclusions are there to guide you even if they are correct a vast majority of the time. Outward attributes you see does not precisely indicate the personal qualities of those around you.

What you see

However, from their outward appearance, some important indicators that tell much about a person's personality are revealed. Part of these indicators includes the cloth they wear, hairstyle, perfume, and some other grooming habits that can be very useful in gaining the right perspective about a particular person. The thing is that many people make use of their style for their outward expression. Although there are some instances in which people dress in a particular way to change their look and probably make some impression that may not correlate to what they are going through internally

A person that has taken the time to look good, presentable, and neat has demonstrated attention to personal appearance to a reasonable extent. On the other hand, people that have an unkempt appearance, display ill social grace.

Does that mean we can judge a person by the kind of clothes they put on alone? No! You need to consider the other variables before you make an erroneous blanket judgment. The only thing is that you can use that to form an initial opinion pending confirmative signs.

What you hear

The way people speak can betray their emotions and show the sort of people they are. People who speak using a steady intonation and a constant, smooth flow of words are typically identified as being self-confident and are at ease in the present circumstances. On the other hand, if you observe that a person has a shaky voice or stutters while addressing you, this can probably indicate the fact that they feel uncomfortable or lack confidence in what is being said. In addition, rapid speech may signify anxiousness or panic.

Apart from the speech pattern itself, there are other variables that can be drawn from how active an individual is during a conversation. The thing is that some people spend most of their time talking and give the person they have a conversion with little or no time to make their own points. Such people may be overconfident, arrogant, or outright rude. They usually have the belief that what they have to say is much more important than what the other person has to say. Other times, it may be the feelings of insecurity that makes them feel they need to overcompensate.

Interesting enough, some research studies show that people that have a loquacious or extroversive nature appear to be more intelligent than they are. But then the supposed intelligence is going to fade out when they make a remark that looks absurd or does not at all appeal to common sense. People that give room for others to express their view have shown reasonable consideration, and the assumption should not be made that the outward projection that is the exact reflection of their internal processes.

What They Listen To

I included this section because a lot of theories seem to revolve around how a person can be analyzed by the kind of music he listens to. Now, there are no definitive explanations for why this is so, but research carried out over the years has shown you can have an idea about the specific traits a certain person has when you check their musical preference.

In a particular study at Heriot-Watt University, the following general traits in people who listen to a specific category of music over a long period of time were theorized.

- Rock: These set of people tend to be creative, gentle, introverted, low self-esteem
- Hip Hop/ Rap: They are not prone to aggression and violence
- Pop: The fans tend to be conventional, honest, high self-esteem and extroverted, the only "but" is that they have relatively little creativity
- Country Music: This set of people are emotionally stable
- Dance: They have an assertive and outgoing personality
- Classical: The listeners are introverted, but then they are comfortable with their skin and have high self-esteem
- Blues/jazz; They tend to be creative, intelligent and extroverted

N.B

By all means, trying to judge a person's traits based on his musical preference is as unscientific as they come. I have included it here mainly for trivial reasons. There is little to suggest that fans of rap are non-violent individuals. Even if the research has shown that most fans of a specific musical genre have certain attributes, not all of them have that trait. Again, nobody has been able to explain the presence or prevalence of certain traits in fans. There is no conclusive evidence that listening to a particular genre will give you certain traits. There is no scientific proof either that having a particular character trait predisposes you to like a particular genre. Cross-sectional studies have shown that certain traits appear more in certain people, but nobody can say for sure what the relationship is. This is one piece of information for the back of your mind. Have it, but its practical value is not high.

Habitual Behavior

As Warren Buffet said, "the chains of habit are too light to be felt until they are too heavy to be broken." The sum total of a person's habits is probably the best indicator yet of their character. After all, our character profile reflects our average attitude and actions.

The habit a person portrays is the most significant indicator of the kind of character they have. For instance, a naturally helpful person may come across as being generous and selfless from the start if they offer to help you out. That alone can communicate that such a person may be empathetic and genuinely caring.

Someone who prefers to stay indoors almost all day may most likely turn out to be highly introverted. That would definitely not be surprising if you find out they enjoy their own company much lot than social gatherings. Someone who literally enjoys hanging out and socializing may be able to make friends more easily than someone who does not. Habits dictate the things we like to do. They facilitate our hobbies and help us avoid boring chores and situations. So, being able to discern a person's habits will give you a huge helping hand in determining just how they think or act.

Another thing to be put into consideration is the particular kind of entertainment that the person enjoys a lot. Some people enjoy sports and games;

others are movie freaks, art lovers, etc. The kind of entertainment a person gets to enjoy can set the tone for his character. A lover of the latest online trends may absolutely love getting new costumes at any cost. The same goes for all the entertainment categories. They can absolutely tell you the hidden truth you want to know about the person.

The Company They Keep

"Show me your friend, and I will tell you who you are."

This highlights how much of an impact the company and relationships we keep have on us. To analyze someone, your work may be made simpler if you know the traits that their closest friends and associates possess. A lot of our habits are picked up subconsciously from the people closest to use. Their traits rub off us and show up in our own life by default. For instance, if you find yourself in the midst of a tightly knit, outward group of friends, that may likely be because you are outgoing yourself. Even if you are not, though, it could mean that you find that trait about them intriguing enough to want to give it a try.

By way of conclusion, there are several pointers that can help you better profile the stranger standing in front of you. If you are able to pin multiple of these pointers in the same direction with regards to certain traits, then you are on safe ground. However, you must be careful not to allow preconceived notions to impede your judgment.

CHAPTER 6:
ANALYZING VERBAL COMMUNICATION

In the previous chapters, a conscious effort has been made to analyze the non-verbal ways of communicating, but then there is a lot to learn from people talking too. I have mentioned something about speech, in fact, but then, as the most important route of communication, it is vital I treat verbal communication as a chapter.

Having said this, you cannot expect people to tell you about their deepest worries or character flaws. However, we can learn a lot by learning to listen and knowing when to speak. Learning to listen beyond the surface is a critical part of verbal communication. For you to make a good analysis about a person, you must make sure you overcome bias when you are listening to them as that will affect your mind and the truth.

Pitch

This is simply a quality of the voice of a person that can be used in determining what other people think about them. The general belief is that women always have a higher-pitched voice, while men consistently have lower pitches. Beyond gender differences, though, low-pitched voices have been connected to calmness, reassurance, and a soothing disposition. This is the very reason why hospitals, call centers, and customer service outfits prefer agents with relatively low-pitched voices.

The pitch of our voice can be controlled in four different ways; chest, nose, mouth, and diaphragm. People that speak with their nose will sound whiny and high-pitched; people that speak with their mouths have lower pitches than them. When you notice someone speaking in a higher pitch than they normally do, it can signify agitation, excitement, or panic.

The majority of the people speak from the chest, and this is to ensure they are being heard. But then, it can later become tiring, and the speaker will have no other choice than to speak with a harsh voice. However, the best place to speak from is the diaphragm. The diaphragm is strong, full, and it requires much training before it can be used effectively. It is also the ultimate if you wish to speak in a pitch that communicates calmness and authority.

Speech Patterns

The speech pattern is simply the way people speak; it's basically how fast the speech is, and the pauses being taken around the flow. For instance, being too fast with your speech makes you look rushed and can be interpreted to mean anxiety. What people will think is that you are probably just pouring out anything that comes out of your mind without even giving thorough thinking to what is coming out of your mouth. While trying to analyze people, be aware that most fast talkers are probably nervous. A lot of people are unable to stop speaking rapidly when they are nervous or anxious.

On the other hand, people that talk with slow, measured pauses sound authoritative, calm, and friendly. Their pattern of speaking indicates that they are taking their time to think about what they have to say before they say it. However, it is important to say that this can be complicated at times because if your speech is too slow, it might be indicating that you are distracted or probably tired. Your audience can get bored if they observe that your speech lacks enthusiasm. Understand that slow speech may be in order to gain more room for thoughts. However, excessively slurred speech can be a precursor of boredom.

Fillers and Pronouns

Does the person you are speaking with use a lot of filler words? What is his pronoun usage like? Does he pause a lot and fill up with unnecessary words?

Fillers are words that break up the normal speech flow without adding any specific meaning to the overall message. Examples of fillers include "like," "um," "uh," "err," and the likes. All fillers have been considered bad lately, and generally, the advice is for people to avoid and get rid of them entirely.

For instance, the repetition of "um" by a speaker points to some level of insecurity, or anxiety. Most of the time, people use fillers when they have stored information with certain pointers. In trying to recollect these pointers, fillers are introduced in place of long, awkward pauses.

The way a person uses pronouns can provide another fascinating insight into his current state of mind. Specifically, the way a person employs and utilizes "You," "I," and "we" can provide an instructive discourse. Usually, when "I" is being employed to convey instructions, it is a message of authority. "I" also provides a dominating and intimidating atmosphere in such case scenarios. "I" is an assertive choice of word, especially when the person addressing you is your superior at work or an older family member. It connotes and denotes a powerful wish when it is used to request for one.

On the other hand, "We" is the safer option people use when they need to carry out a task, they find distasteful. "We" could also be used to mitigate the potential impact of the news about to be delivered. It is easier to hide behind "We" when firing someone, for instance. It is always, "We cannot continue to employ you," as opposed to using "I." It can also be a route to escape responsibility for a transgression or unpleasant task. In short, "we" comes in pretty handy when you want to communicate that a situation is out of your hands. However, when "We" does not refer to a single entity or organization, it can be an indicator of "togetherness," especially in unheated situations. Romantic arrangements are a notable example of this.

The use of "You" is particularly complex. It all depends on the context and pitch of the speaker. "You" can be made to sound accusatory under the right situations. A speaker that emphasizes "You" may be trying to pass a message of non-involvement or non-consent. "You," though, can also be made to sound placatory. However, most of the time, "You" is a message of dissociation; people use it frequently in a conversation to make it clear that they are a separate entity from the other party. Learn to notice when "You" is accusatory. Pair its use with other visual clues such as frowns or scowls.

CONCLUSION

In trying to understand people better, it is important to be able to understand personality type and current emotional state. Just knowing what a person's mood is currently is enough to help you pick up cues that will help your conversation flow better. That means you will be consistently and constantly one step ahead in the conversation. That means you can spot even narcissistic traits a mile away. It means you can spot holes when someone is trying to hoodwink you.

It is not enough to just speak; you also need to be able to understand what people say to you and even what they have left unsaid. It is not enough to converse with the people around you; it is better if you can actually understand them and the motivation that drives them at that point. That is the greatest gift you can give yourself in social gatherings.

Learn to understand body language. Allow your conversations to go beyond just the verbal aspect;

there are so many more dimensions to communication. Allow yourself the best chance of having fruitful conversations by joining the less than one percent of people who truly understand body language. Begin to hear not just the words directed at you but the body language behind them.

Analyzing people, the right way will save you a ton of trouble, help you communicate better, and keep you one step ahead in your conversations!

HOW TO ANALYZE PEOPLE:

Why is there so much conflict in personal communication?

Well, the answer is simple. Too many people do not hear beyond the words directed at the[m]. Unable to reconcile the message in these words with what they suspect/perceive, conflict ensue[s]

Ninety percent of people leave their minds on autopilot. Most people hear what is said to them a[nd] have no choice but to accept because they do not have the mental ability to examine the words a[nd] match it with or against the body language being displayed. Others can notice body language cu[es] but cannot interpret them.

How would you like to be able to understand body language better?

Here is the good news; you can learn to read and understand body language cues. Yes, you do n[ot] need specialized training to be able to understand what people say and what they leave unsaid.

Some of the topics that you will get to learn about include:

- Explains the nexus between values, belief system, and attitude
- Helps you understand your attitude as a prerequisite for understanding others
- Throws more light on some of the most common body language cues
- Teaches you to analyze speech patterns
- Explains seven compelling reasons why you should learn to analyze people
- Shows a practical way to validate what a person says with what their body says
- Traces the origins of the different character profile and attitude people have

Communication can be confusing or feel incomplete. By applying the tips in this book, you will [be] empowered to fill in the gaps of communication and be able to communicate better. Understand t[he] underlying sentiments driving the person in front of you and adjust accordingly. Imagine being ab[le] to tell when people are not entirely truthful or trying to hide something from you. I can attest to th[is] making life much easier.

Analyzing people isn't the rocket science that it is purported to be. It can be easy if you know t[he] right things to do. Are you interested in communicating and understanding people better?

Get this book today to discover the secrets of analyzing people.

ISBN 978-82-93738-26[8]

9 788293 738268

EVIL PORTENT
James Field
Life in the Clouds - Book#4